The Primer on Du Jenseits and the assfucking sex

Revised & Updated Second Edition

Du

First Edition Copyright © 2018 Du. All rights reserved.
This, Revised & Updated Second Edition Copyright © 2019 Du. All rights reserved.

ISBN: 978-0-359-77541-5 (Lulu-assigned)

Publisher: Du

Categories: Non-Classifiable
       Nonfiction > Philosophy > General
Proposed Classification: Nonfiction > Just Talking > Plain Talking

About the Author/ Author's Note

Du is now, by Deed Poll, my legal name, since October 2002. 2019, late sixties.

Schizophrenic by professional qualification, free man by occupation, happy by orientation, dreamer by choice.

I have lived all my life in Singapore, but I have memory of having been around a little, on both the Du side of things, and the Not-Du side of things, before coming into this world, and so, I am NOT so easily fooled by this little world, and its story, on the Not-Du side of things.

I am fast on my way out of this little world, and I want plain talking when it comes to the serious matter, namely, **Du Jenseits and the assfucking sex**. This volume is THE most important of all my books, the rest are NOT important, just talking shop, talking idle straws in the wind.

Preface

The essentials about **Du Jenseits, and the assfucking sex**, the absolute basics. **'Du'** [doo] means 'you', **'Jenseits'** [YEN-zytes] means 'That Side', as in German.

Only the first two poems are pre-requisite reading and constitute the 'official' writeup on **Du Jenseits and the assfucking sex**. The rest of The Primer helps to fill out the picture a little.

Based on what come, what take, this primer serves as an introduction and re-awakening to **Du Jenseits and the assfucking sex**, which, as far as I'm concerned, and as far as I can see, refers to what's for real, after all,?, and is the serious matter, when it comes to what is really important, to one and all.

I want plain talking, don't I?

Anyway, Where do you think you are going?, what do you suppose? – the old question. You again?

Where do you think you are going?,
what do you suppose?
-- the old question.
You again?

"On a clear day, you can see forever"

The Essentials, About Du Jenseits and the assfucking sex

"All based on German"

My father, the MC, said:
"All based on German.
All speak English.
It is too wicked to speak German so properly under the heat of the day."

Come clean on the English tongue, and I shall see if you make sense
'**Du**' means 'you'
Correct, proceed apace

Du has nothing to do with German, way, way, way beyond German
Just happens, along the way,
'**Du**' means 'you',
As in the German in this little world, and all

I don't care for the ambivalent Norwegian 'De eller du', 'De or du'
Let alone the Punjabi 'du' meaning 'she',
And all is more lost at sea

Don't dare translate these two words:
'**Du**' (doo), meaning 'you', and '**Jenseits**' (YEN-zytes), meaning 'That Side'
The rest are NOT that important
But, you should know about and address
The assfucking sex, Arschficksex, the bottomline, the live wire

That's all I know and or care to take, --
These three things:
1. The assfucking sex;
2. Du;
3. Jenseits
All manner of false Du's, all manner of false Jenseits's

All manner of false assfucking sex,es
Confusion doubly confounded, compoundedly confounded, and all
Let alone the Not-Du side of things
NOT Du, I am NOT interested
My veesh is my command

'Jenseits' means 'That Side', 'beyond, yonder, yonsides'
And refers to
What's for real, after all
Was heißt wirklich immerhin
Where the substance is
Where it's all there oledy doch schon

Like my father, the MC, said:
"Jenseits, that's where you really are.
Diesseits, you are just a shadow of yourself.
Anything that makes you unhappy, can't be."

"All based on German", so see

If you say 'you', for example,
You get confined to a little pink quarter in the middle of nowhere
You say **'Du',**
Then you get it all
'Du' the one word to it all

'Life' the one word to it all, says English,
Including Death, God, and the devil, and all
No larger than Life?
No John Wayne to shoot up the town, none?
I beg to differ
'Life' the one word to it all, says English
Trust the English test
And English has failed the English test, by me

If, again, you say 'That Side',
You don't make it to even

Happy Hunting Ground on the Red Indian's count
Let alone let alone let alone

The stupid local Germans of, in this little world
Say 'Jenseits', yes, but by 'Jenseits'
They simply mean, if you ask them, 'beyond the grave'
But, **Jenseits** is
A long, long, long way to go
NOT that long, that's all

The Christian Heaven again, igen?
Just the kindergarten play, still?
I want plain talking
One man's dream is another man's delusion
What's for real, after all?
Was heißt wirklich immerhin?
Doch!?

Oh yeah, you know everything, if you so damn smart, where were you before you were born?

Du, D-yoU, stupid!, where do you think you are going?, what do you suppose?, as we were wont to say in yester,hell,s, now don't you remember, or something, and then what? --

Ah ain't seen nothin' yet, ach!, so……..?

Focus Partner
Simple
Einfach
, as the oldtimers in yester,hell,s were saying...

Jenseits
, wieder 'rueck, immer noch besser,
den ganzen Weg, doch schon

To brighter shores and healthier climes,
All THE way
immer noch besser,

den ganzen Weg
Can't miss

All in good order, all in good time
Can't miss

Can't miss

Ah ain't seen nothin' yet, ach!, so........?

Jenseits
so so so so so so so
mm

so,

currently, still, in deep shits, what prevailing nightmare, and all
Just the cheebyefucking conbobulations only
Just the little anthill,
Including all the hitherto seen

so komm, so komm
so komm nicht, so komm nicht
so komm, so komm

What come, what take

what blip on the radar:
mm pak k'ũah tiok-eh liau,
den Herzuvorungeshen,d,en,
the hitherto unseen,
what compound male conbobulations
was immer noch auch SO

Beyond this Just the little anthill,
Including the mudflats, and all, --
What vast expanses way, way, way beyond, and all, aiowno
Du, absolutely mindboggling, way, way, way beyond imagination, and all,

Let alone
J e n s e i t s
so komm nicht, so komm nicht
so
mm pak k'ũah tiok-eh liau
what compound male conbobulations
was immer noch auch SO
so komm nicht, so komm nicht
so
was immer noch auch s o   ,?

Now you are current with me
As of today, 23 February 2018
Singapore

Anyway,

Where do you think you are going?,
what do you suppose?
-- the old question.

You again?

What come, what take

Cheebyedom only, so far
Big fat deal, no big deal

The clean ones, no less
The Waterfall, for some encouragement
So happy, no less
Who knows what even better yet,!,?
No headway
But,
The clean ones, no less
The Waterfall, for some encouragement

Current, as of 7 July 2019, Singapore

What have you got?, or, Enumerations and Ruminations

What does **Jenseits** have?

Should like to compare field notes with
Anyone happens to be in town
Worth his salt, at least half a pinch

Let's see what I've got:

All the assfucking sex in all of forever
Partner will be there
There will be Company
What sex in the sun, and all
Was für Sex im Sonne,
und so weiter,
was immer noch auch so

Men's black cock hair im Umwelt

Shiffe
Ozean
Was für Luft
ach, so
Was zum Freude

Piddle
Assfucking
Cocksucking

Arsefuck
Lovemake

Lifesex
Realplay
Forces' games
Arsefuck for Arsefuck selbst

Travel
Sports
Forces' games

Walking, talking, seeing
Singing, dancing
Poetry, music

Some superorgasmic Big Bang
Auf dem Vereinigung?

First Class
The permanent population
Permanent body
Forever, without beginning, without end,
as always, fuer immer, Forever,
one day at a time, every new day, or something,
Forever

Lower Classes, down through Fifth Class,
What new life meant to be,
New generation every new day,
But, always First Class come down, but NEVER in the flesh,
All the way back First Class,
Otherwise NOT even absolutely nothing below,
And even that is **Du**
At the end of each new day,
Im Herzen, alles gut und KLAR doch schon

First Class forever
Lower Classes unmissable

"Always hometown"?
At least in Lower Classes,

There be cities, and all
Cars, planes, trains, ships, motorbikes

Throughout the Classes,
"Sun, world, ocean, edge of the world
Edge of the edge of the world
All fall into place, in a life that's full
And all because of you, and only you"

Assfucking manforms assfucking assfucking manforms, non-stop
Like breathing out, and breathing in

A voll (full) and varied life all based on assfucking sex, and **Du**

What about you?
What have you got?

You again?

Anyway,

Where do you think you are going?,
what do you suppose?
-- the old question.

You again?

The Primer Continuing

The Wizard of Oz Came One

The Wizard of Oz came one I find of use:
"Somewhere over the rainbow, way up high
There's a land that I heard of once, in a lullaby..."

Alice in Winter Wonderland
Found there were only men around
At any rate, manforms
Assfucking manforms assfucking assfucking manforms,
And hit on the Eureka!:
"Why did my mother never tell me so!?"

She wriggled through the rabbit hole
Leading through to a clear patch
And saw the Wizard of Oz
Spinning his lifelong tale
And queried of him:
"But, Wizard, aren't you happy?"

The Wizard sang his telling song
And the Witchet of Oz canted:
"And merry little England shall never know
Happiness the English end.
Cast a spell on you."
But, Alice was unflinching and determined
To take the Wizard of Oz's song
Back
To the world

And that's how I, Mannkey,
Got to hear it
And it is the signature tune of

Mannkey's Happy Dream

"Somewhere over the rainbow, way up high
There's a land that I heard of once, in a lullaby..."

So the sexual economy, so the economic economy,...so the economy

Like my father, the MC, was asking:
"Who are they?"
So, Who are they?
That's Who are they?
The haves

On the Du side of things,
They are called
An what motley band only
Upon the Ugly Truth about Du
Have
What assfucking sex what count, and all
The rest can go to Hell,
As far as I am concerned
So the sexual economy, so the economic economy,
so the political economy, so the social economy, so the economy

On the Not-Du side of things,
They are called
What's for real, after all, ones
Have
What's for real, after all,
Assfucking sex, and all
The assfucking sex, they claim, is all theirs
Like my father, The Papa-Thing, their spokesman, said
Of the have-not upstarts, like the common gays in this little world:
"Slaughter them! They want it, right? Slaughter them!"

So the sexual economy, so the economic economy,...so the economy

Like my father, the MC, said:
"You are you, and they are they"

Both these groups or bands can come up with only Hermaphroditicisms

Like my father, the MC, said:
"They don't want so he,
They want a touch of she"

That's all the economy can afford

So the story goes

I don't entertain failure

An what motley band only
Upon the Ugly Truth about Du,
On the Du side of things,
For All' Diesseits This Absolutely Only One Time In Forever,
At least in these immediate quarters,
Just answer to, the question:

was alle   ,!,?

(what all   ,!,?)

What I still say is:
What Ugly Truth about Du?
No wart in the heart
What sexual economy...?
It's just a skeleton in Du's cupboard,
It's NOT Du's skeleton, is it?
Like my father, the MC, said:
"No tail"

Never so hard-up
Never so silly
Never so weak-minded, so see

Ah ain't seen nothin' yet, ach!, so……..?

What My Father, the MC, Said

My father, the MC, said:
"Jenseits
Never so weak-minded,
That's all we can say,
Too weak-minded to put it any better."
When I asked my father,
What about Diesseits?
My father, the MC, simply said:
"Shadow-boxing."

My father, the MC, said:
"Jenseits, that's where you really are.
Diesseits, you are just a shadow of yourself.
Anything that makes you unhappy, can't be."

When I asked my father
Where Jenseits was,
He said:
"Don't know.
But, simply say,
Where the substance is."

But, if you keep saying,
Substance, substance, substance,
You are likely to fly into a white wall.

So, what I simply say is:
Jenseits refers to
What's for real, after all,
Was heißt wirklich immerhin,

Where the substance is,
Where it's all there oledy doch schon

The Kabuki Boys

In yesterhells, there was once when when the kabuki boys
Were performing with their sex overlord,
With breath control and breathing rhythmic techniques, and all,
As they assfucked with their sex overlord while performing kabuki dance,
They decided to teach the women a lesson
And sent the women there tumbling backwards into water jars
The kabuki boys, with their sex overlord, blithely carried on
While each time the women regained their balance
They were sent tumbling backwards to the water jars
This continued for eons on end
So that the women vowed that given half the chance
They would NOT seek death
But annihilation

Eventually, somehow the women had their chance
And they walked through the Forest of Annihilation
Till they surfaced as Staff,
One of the sex overlords,
Who said, talking to himself practically:
"There, it's only you, after all"
The women had their wish

That's, however, NOT the end of the story,
At least, I hope NOT
"Gone without his supper!",
Like Father Ash?
I still insist:
Can't miss
All in good order, all in good time
Can't miss

Can't miss

The Song of My Heart

Thunder thighs and bronze buttocks that enable me to breathe
"A thing of beauty is a joy forever"
You are the apple of my eye
The whole man and his visage, eye to eye
Men may come, and men may go
In the shifting sands of what new life meant to be
The rock that stays says at end of day
You are the only one left for me
In 'the culture of desire'
It's you alone who light my fire
A fire that burns for forever
The sun to all and sundry
When we have sex in the sun with Company
Even then, it's only you that I see
What you see is what you fuck
And you are what you fuck
So, you my identity, sexual and all
How can I miss in Arschficksex, withal?
Sun, world, ocean, edge of the world
Edge of the edge of the world
All fall into place in a life that's full
And all because of you, and only you
The mystery of life bears no light
Where the wonder of you shines like the noonday sun
"But, most of all I love you 'cause you're you"
The song of my heart throughout, -- that's Du

Das Lied meines Herzens

Donnerschenkel und Bronzengesäß, der mir zu atmen möglich machen
„Ein Ding der Schönheit ist eine Freude für immer"
Du bist der Apfel meines Auges
Der ganze Mann und sein Antlitz, Auge zu Auge
Männer mögen kommen, und Männer mögen gehen
In den sich verschiebenden Sanden von was neuem Leben zu sein gemeint
Der Fels, der bleibt, sagt am Tagesende
Bist Du den Einzigen für mich übrig gelassen
In „dem Kultur des Begierdes",
Ist es Du allein, der meinen Feuer anzündet
Ein Feuer, der für immer brennt
Der Sonne allen und den mehreren
Wann wir im Sonne mit Company Sex haben,
Sogar dann ist es Du allein, den ich sehe
Was du siehst, ist was du fickst
Und du bist, was du fickst
So, Du mein Identität, sexuell und alle
Wie kann ich verfehlen im Arschficksex, insgesamt?
Sonne, Welt, Ozean, Weltsseite, Weltsseitesseite
Alles in Platz fallen, in einem Leben, das voll ist
Und all wegen dein, und dein allein
Das Lebensrätsel trägt kein Licht,
Wo der Wunder von Du wie der Mittagssonne scheint
„Aber meist vor allem liebe ich dich, weil du du bist"
Das Lied meines Herzens durchaus, das heißt, -- Du

It's the Person you want in the end, isn't it?

It's the Person you want in the end, isn't it?

'Person' and 'personality' from 'per sona',
The Latin for 'through the sound'
As Gonzales was saying:
"It's through the sound that I know who you are"

If the assfucking sex is all you want!?
Don't be silly!

It's the Person you want in the end, isn't it?

I might say, the purpose of life is:
It's only for you that I live,
And I live to assfuck with you
But, it's the Person you want in the end, isn't it?

Love, the one thing that holds it all together for you,
In conjunction with Company,
Between you and your Partner.
Forever

But, what is a man to do with his wife,
If she loves him for only his wealth,
Professional qualifications, power or social status,
But NOT for himself?
Or, what is God to do with you,
If you love Him for only His glory
Or the chance to share in His eternal life,

But NOT for Himself?

It's the Person you want in the end, isn't it?
"Till the stars all burn away
And he'll be there"
For you

It's the Person you want in the end, isn't it?

Jenseitsbound

There was a time
When I knew what happiness was
My heart was full
And all was in place

Now come Diesseits
And I'm all alone
With only the shadows to bother me
Myself NOT half the man I used to be

Back home to you
Where Company also is
Back Jenseits
In a jiff

Piddle, and the Current

Piddle is:
Upon through-body rear-entry anal intromission,
So that the two bodies are together as one,
Both facing the same direction,
Cock rub cock,
Balls roll balls,
With the assfucking motion in the rectum still ongoing,
Courtesy of the current

You don't have piddle in this little world,
Or likely ever able to,
This little world, what hardtack reality, and all,
On the Not-Du side of things,
Where anal-penetrative intercourse is painful, and all

Beyond this little world,
On the Du side of things,
Where it's assfucking manforms assfucking assfucking manforms,
Non-stop,
Piddle is deemed first prize,
Assfucking, second,
And cocksucking, third

My father, the MC, once instructed me in yesterhells,
How when you walk-piddle, piddle-walk,
And you want to assfuck,
You seize off, with your sex partner,
Then the two bodies come apart,
And you can then fuck arse, one on one

With piddle, and the current,

You can see how any number of manforms can come together,
Whether strung out in a line with the assfucking bodies filtering one through another,
Or, all piled up together,
Like six million men in a phone booth,
All assfucking,
And walking as one man

Walking, in those areas of Life,
On the Du side of things,
Always entailed piddling,
With the assfucking sex motion ongoing non-stop,
Courtesy of the current,
Which current is also absent in this world,
On the Not-Du side of things,
Where the kind of walking one does,
Without the piddle-assfuck current,
Is called by my father, the MC,
"Dry walking"

My father, the MC, was saying:
"Walk, don't run, now only dry walking.
When return you the current,
You can fly like the wind."

"The shock will kill you"

My father, the MC, said:
"The shock will kill you"

He was referring to
Your shock on seeing
The whole sky an embankment of
Assfucking manforms assfucking assfucking manforms,
All muscular, well-shaped, bronzed and beautiful,
And all assfucking,
One behind the other,
Live wire, with current, and all...

Ah ain't seen nothin' yet, ach!, so........?

Now You See It, Now You Don't

The assfucking sex

So, you don't want it
But, the haves,
Especially the What's for real, after all, ones,
Just have what they have,
And, ever so often, if indeed insist
On flashing it to you,
And you in turn can't quite let it go altogether,
But keep looking up back at it
Now you see it, now you don't

I spied a sea of ocean floors

When in yester,hell,s they did indeed
Find beneath the veneer of salt water and seaweed
The invisible but palpably physical, --
The motley few skindivers given some visuals, --
Assfucking manforms assfucking assfucking manforms
Chock block and in serration
On the sea floor,
Lying lethargic, waiting for the start of things

Wonder, though, what there be, what gives
In the Ocean
Assfucking manforms assfucking assfucking manforms
Action
Same as everywhere
Then, what?

Wonder what Jenseits has
For activity,ies in the World,
Let alone the Ocean,
Let alone let alone the Sun, and all,
Though I have some inkling more about the Sun
Than about the Ocean,
What purposive activity,ies beyond, possibly, forces' games...?

Wondrous mysterious
And invitingly enticing
A happy thought thereto
Betimes, betides
What mells if not tells

Ὁ δόρμο μοῦ εἶναι κοντά τῆς θάλασσα
O dhórmo moo eeneh kontáh tis tháhlahssah

My house is near the sea
How First Class at Partnerplatz,
The twain carry on by the Ocean side

"Du's Ocean is empty"
versus
"Look at the oceans, teeming with life!"
But, manforms galore all happily assfucking
That be what be in Du's Ocean, and more

The, Basic, Principles of Prussian Upbringing, and of Du and Duology

Like my father, the MC, said:
"The love is there."
And positive thinking is essential.
But, for Selbst, Self, you have Wertschätzung, esteem
Partner, Liebe, love
And Company, Hochachtung, regard

Just as with Selbst, Self, you have Wohlsein, wellbeing
Partner, Happiness, happiness
And Company, Freude, joy

And by Selbst, Self, you have Stolz, pride
Partner, Zucht, breed, culture, discipline, sexual uprightness, propriety, properness
And Company, Pflicht, duty

These are the basic principles of Prussian upbringing,
And hold, as such, for Du and Duology, at least generally speaking, so far...
'**Du**' means 'you', as in the German of this little world...

With the assistance of the websites:
wie-sagt-man-noch.de and dict.cc,
I have been able to work out
Further developments for the paradigm:

From Selbst, Self, you have Selbsterfüllung, self-fulfilment
From Partner, Personesalter, Personhood
From Company, Gesellschaft, company

In Selbst, Self, you have Individualität, individuality
In Partner, Identität, identity
In Company, Universalität, universality

By Selbst, Self, you have Befertigung, Vorbereitung, preparation
With Partner, Vereinigung, consummation, union
In Company, Umgehung, circulation

By Selbst, Self, you have Körper,Pflege, grooming
With Partner, Liebesmachen, lovemaking
In Company, Freilaufen, freewheeling

By Selbst, Self, you have Souveränität, sovereignty
With Partner, Eigentum, property, ownership
In Company, Gemeinschaftsgeist, esprit de corps, camaraderie

...

Hab' doch 'was Du Sinn   !

Mit Tränen weinen...
OHNE Tränen weinen,
Dann komm man auf den Arschficksexsinn

It ain't even German, none, let alone germaine,!,
well, I'll be fucked most unclean chapcheng cheebye
just like Hitler so   ,!

Through the morass,
Heading through the hitherto unseen

mm pak k'ũah tiok-eh liau
what compound male conbobulations
was immer noch auch SO

Not yet male, how to talk?
was immer noch auch SO
That's how

Not yet male, what to say?
So shut up!
So shut me up, none
Shut up, little fellow   ,!

Anyway,

Where do you think you are going?,
        what do you suppose?
            -- the old question.

You again?

Hab' doch 'was Du Sinn   !

Wohin denkst du, daß du gehst?,
        was nimmst du an?
              -- die alte Frage.

Du noch mal?

Where do you think you are going?,
        what do you suppose?
              -- the old question.

You again?

If a nightmare is all you care to make of it?
I'd rather, Dare to to have a happy dream
Can't miss
You make your own bed
Tang kau laih kay, lah!
Wait till come still, lah!
Tang kau laih kay, lah!
All in good order, all in good time
Can't miss

What come, what take

The clean ones, no less
The Waterfall, for some encouragement
So happy, no less
Who knows what even better yet,!,?
No headway
But,
The clean ones, no less
The Waterfall, for some encouragement
Soweit (thus far)
Nur soweit (only so far)
Current, 7 July 2019, Singapore

Something tells, this is it
This time for real, and all

NOT allowed to mess around so much

NOT allowed to mess around so much
Now you know too damn well, or something
Take it from there, see how

Jenseits (YEN-zytes), That Side, beyond, yonder, yonsides,
Where you really are,
Where it's all there oledy doch schon,
All as clear as day,
Everything in order,
Alles in Ordnung,
Alles gut und klar doch schon

Diesseits (DEES-zytes), This Side,
All' Diesseits This Absolutely Only One Time In Forever,
Where you are just a shadow of yourself,
Messing around in the dark, and all,
You can have it any way you want
All the topsyturviness, disorder and new-fangled jambalaya
Like your being a woman or fish
It's all only shadow-boxing
Nothing lost, nothing gained
But, just the same,
NOT allowed to mess around so much
Now you know too damn well, or something
Take it from there, see how

It's all up to Jenseits really, to reveal all, if so, and all...
Can't miss

Ah ain't seen nothin' yet, ach!, so……..?

Jenseits
so so so so so so so
mm

So,

Where do you think you are going?,
what do you suppose?
-- the old question.

You again?

One Heart

My father, the MC, said:

"We're all the same boat."

My father, the MC, said:

"One heart."

My father, the MC, said:

"Missed two beats."

Musik und Musikanten, Die,

Wagner
Allein
Voraus soher
Ausständig
„Morgentlich leuchtend im rosigen Schein"
Des Preislieds von *Den Meistersingern von Nürnberg*
Die erste Linie allein
So von Jenseits, so von Jenseits, was?
Ähnlich

Frei, freilig, feierlig
Haydn
Der österreichische kaiserliche Seliganthem,
Das Lied der Deutschen
Schubert
So komm bei mir einst,mal
...

Jetzt,?
Ungekannt
Klavier
Schön
„Ich danke dir,"
Himmlische, heilige, heile Kunst,
Du Kunst,
So gehörig und heimig auch

„Morgentlich leuchtend im rosigen Schein"

„Morgentlich leuchtend im rosigen Schein"
ach, so
Nur solch ein kleiner „ach, so"
ach, so, ach, so
was immer noch auch so

Österreichische Leichtlieferungen, and Strauss

was tun?, was tun?, was tun?
österreichische Leichtlieferungen, wie immer noch auch so,!
alles, was Schatten so können
so erlaubt
so komm
so sollen?

Like "Americans speak English after a fashion"
Austrians speak German after a fashion
Then, too, uniquely:
Like All' Diesseits This Absolutely Only One Time In Forever
To Jenseits
Nur ein' halbe Chance, oder?, noch?
Only half a chance, or something?, still?

Schubert allein kam einst,mal
meinenwegs, meinetwegs
deutsch so deutsch, was?

Stets aber der Strauß allein
Tales from the Vienna Woods,
Märchen aus den Wienerwäldern
Roses from the South, Rosen aus dem Süden
Emperor Waltz, Kaiserswalzer
Morning Paper Waltz, Morgenzeitungswalzer, Morgenblattwalzer
Vienna Bonbons, Wienerbonbons
Voices of Spring, Frühlingsstimmen
And, of course,
On the banks of the Beautiful Blue Danube,
An der schönen blauen Donau

And, I hear, they play
The *Blue Danube Waltz*
Every hour on the hour
Every New Year's Day
In Austria or Vienna
Kinda apt, don't you think?

When Du sounds more like Du to me,
If only "after a fashion"

"I can smile at the old days,
It was beautiful then
I remember the time I knew what happiness was"...

A little mouse's prayer of thanksgiving

Thanks, Jenseits
In all of forever, there is Du
Thanks, Du, for Du
>Du<

A little mouse's prayer of thanksgiving

ach, so

That's how Germans talk
Don't need translation, right?
Don't be so stupid
Don't be so crazy
Don't be so silly
Just don't be silly anymor-e,!
Go by ear, see how

...

Yé Xiáng Lăi, von der Nacht gedacht, Thought From The Night

Yé xiáng lăi
von der Nacht gedacht
Thought from the night

Ōtōkō-nō si mannkey...
Năn jì

Dào lė zhèi bù
Zhèng huěi yī bù
Zhèng bù guò lė
Bù bù jìn bù

Mannes Tod Mannkey Traum...
Mannes Aufmerkung, des Männlichen Aufmerkung,
Mann erinnert sich, der Männliche erinnert sich

Auf diesen Schritt erreichen haben
Einen Schritt, auf dem wirklichen Wiederzurrueckkehr
Den wirklichen Schritt, vorbei
Schritt für Schritt, immer noch besser

Man's death mannkey dream...
Man's register, The male's register,
Man remembers, The male remembers

Having reached this step
One step, in getting back this time for real
Past the real step
Step by step, get to improve, ever better

Looking Ahead

Something tells, this is it
This time for real, and all

Where the men are

What compound male conbobulations,
and all

So far from it all
So happy, no less

Who knows what even better yet!?
But, of course!
Doch!, was?
But, of course!

immer noch besser,!

The clean ones, no less
The Waterfall, for some encouragement
So happy, no less
Who knows what even better yet,!,?
No headway
But,
The clean ones, no less
The Waterfall, for some encouragement